First published in Great Britain in 1988
by Hutchinson Children's Books
An imprint of Century Hutchinson Ltd
Brookmount House, 62-65 Chandos Place,
Covent Garden, London WC2N 4NW

Century Hutchinson Australia (Pty) Ltd
16-22 Church Street, Hawthorn, Melbourne, Victoria 3122

Century Hutchinson New Zealand Limited
32-34 View Road, PO Box 40-086, Glenfield, Auckland 10

Century Hutchinson South Africa (Pty) Ltd
PO Box 337, Bergvlei 2012, South Africa

Set in Linotron Palatino
Design/typesetting by Roger Walker Graphic Design

Printed and bound in Portugal by Printer Portuguesa

British Library Cataloguing in Publication Data
West, Colin
    Trotting off to market.
    I. Title
    823'.914[J]
ISBN 0-09-173676-5

# Trotting off to market

## Colin West

## Hutchinson

London Melbourne Auckland Johannesburg

One morning Mrs Trotter
Appealed to little Sam:
'Please trot along to market
And fetch a pot of jam.'

So Sam, he took a sixpence,
And thought, 'How grand I am!
I'm trotting off to market
To buy a pot of jam.'

And when he'd trotted halfway,
Who should he meet but Ned,
Who asked where he was off to,
So this is what he said:

'I'm trotting off to market
To buy my mum a pot;
A pot of . . . . Goodness Gracious!
I can't remember what!'

Said Ned, 'A pot of fish paste?'
Said Sam, 'No, I think not.'

Said Ned, 'A pot of mustard?'
'No Ned, but thanks a lot.'

As Sam he trotted onwards,
Who should he meet but Sue,
Who asked where he was off to,
So Sam, he answered true:

'I'm trotting off to market
To buy my mum a pot;
A pot of something sticky,
But I've forgotten what.'

Said Sue, 'A pot of honey?'
Said Sam, 'No, I think not.'

Said Sue, 'A pot of treacle?'
'No Sue, but thanks a lot.'

As Sam he trotted onwards,
Who should he meet but Ben,
Who asked where he was off to,
So Sam said yet again:

'I'm trotting off to market
To buy my mum a pot;
A pot of something special,
But I've forgotten what.'

Said Ben, 'A pot of coffee?'
Said Sam, 'No, I think not.'

Said Ben, 'A pot of pepper?'
'No Ben, but thanks a lot.'

As Sam he trotted onwards,
He thought, 'How sad I am.
I'm really in a pickle
And I'm really in a jam!'

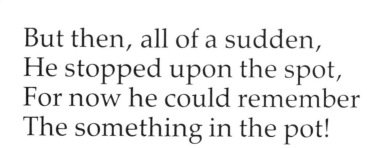

But then, all of a sudden,
He stopped upon the spot,
For now he could remember
The something in the pot!

'Hooray!' he sang out, loudly,
And cried, 'how glad I am
That I'm not in a pickle
And I'm not in a jam!'

Sam trotted off to market
As fast as he could trot,
And there he spent his sixpence
And bought – can you guess what?

Sam trotted back from market,
But look at what he's got!
He trotted back to Mother
With PICKLE in a pot!